ACKNOWLEDGMENTS

I would like to thank my wife Laura; my daughters Ashley, Allyssa, and Sara Grace; and my sons-in-law Andrew and Dan for all of their support and encouragement throughout the process! I love you all very much.

Special thanks goes out to my editor Eric Strobel. Eric...you are an amazing person! So capable, talented, and patient. Thanks for your excellent work. You are the best! Annie McNeill, your artistic design talents are a gift, thank you for your willingness to share your abilities on the cover design!

D1708655

i

TABLE OF CONTENTS

INTRODUCTION

One of the first relationship patterns I experienced as a counselor when I started in the mental health field more than 25 years ago was one person being a bit controlling and the other having a desire to please. One person needing to be right and the other person needing to be liked. I remember working with a young couple who we will call "Bob and Beth." They were entering counseling early on in their relationship because Beth was getting a bit stressed by Bob's moods. Beth, as most co-dependents do, minimized the issue but just wanted to talk it through for one session with a professional. Bob thought the need for the counseling session was ridiculous and that Beth was overreacting and taking things way too personally. Needless to say, the counseling lasted only for a session for Bob while Beth continued individual counseling for over two years as she started to realize how invalidating and controlling Bob was. She began to understand that by continuing to endure this pattern, she was actually contributing to the problem.

This pattern continues to be one of the main problems in dating, marital, and familial relationships that I see as a counselor. Sometimes a relationship starts with both a narcissistic and a very dependent person, but more often than not it consists of a controlling and a pleasing person, Bob and Beth respectively. BUT…as their dance continues, it often evolves into an even more dysfunctional situation of the controlling person becoming anywhere from mildly to severely narcissistic and the pleaser becoming mildly to severely codependent. This is what I refer to as the "dance" throughout this book. My use of the term "dance" is not intended to minimize or ridicule the situation. Rather; I have found that the interactions between a narcissistic personality and a co-dependent resembles a dance because the situation requires two participants and requires a give and take between the two; much like a dance.

I will first spend time discussing the origins and definitions of narcissism and codependency. Next, I will focus on some of the early stages of the "dance". I will then move into what eventually happens in the dance including a focus on family dynamics and the impact of the dance on the next generation … the couple's children. The book will then focus on the key antidotes for the "dance" including specific steps for the narcissist, co-dependent, parents, children, and adult children needed to break out of the cycle.

CHAPTER 1

NARCISSISM...WHAT IT IS & WHAT IT IS NOT

Throughout my professional practice, the word narcissism has been used often, and in a wide variety of ways. Like so many other clinical terms, terms like "bipolar" or "OCD" or "ADHD", narcissism is not understood very well. Lay people often use these clinical terms as shorthand for unattractive personality traits. For example, if someone knows a person who is a bit selfish, they may call him or her a "narcissist." The selfish person may or may not actually satisfy the clinical definition of "narcissist." The misuse of the clinical term as a pejorative often causes confusion and resentment. Narcissism is truly a condition that resides on a spectrum, ranging from mild on one end to severe at the other. For the purpose of this book, I would like to go over the most common symptoms of narcissistic personality disorder and talk about how they take shape in a person and in the contexts of relationships with a codependent and others.

If someone has a personality disorder, it usually means that their symptoms have been fully integrated into their personality, resulting in the development of a chronic, unhealthy pattern of behaving. In order for someone to meet the clinical criteria for narcissistic personality disorder, they have to have at least five of the following nine symptoms:

1. Exaggerates Achievements & Talents...A Grandiose Sense of Self-Importance

You and I probably have known someone who fits into this category! This is the person who after a round of golf says they got a certain score and you know for a FACT that they did much worse. They also tend to bring stories about you and I back to themselves in a "one up you" sort of way in order to bring attention to themselves. I've often said in my seminars that a true narcissist's capacity to love others is not nearly as great as their need to be loved by others.

As we will find with most of the symptoms of narcissism, the origin of this symptom is often an upbringing featuring parental neglect, abandonment, or significant shame. A shaming parent tends to tell his or her child that they will never measure up, will look at what they aren't versus what they are, and will tend to control the child through poor emotional regulation. When a child has a poor attachment with a parent either through neglect, abandonment or shame, they tend to compensate for this by withdrawing into their own world or bullying others in the same way that they were bullied by the shaming parent.

An alternative basis for this symptom is a highly entitled upbringing. One feature of this type of upbringing is a sense that one's personal failures are always someone else's fault ... the coach, the faith community, the teacher, the friend; and they tend to always get what they want. When someone lives and breathes this style for years they will expect to be acknowledged for things that are greater than what they did and will expect to be seen as the most important person in the room. They will often show this by demanding to be acknowledged because they consider themselves to be all that really matters.

The table is being set for a later symptom which we will discuss - the lack of empathy.

2. Preoccupation with Fantasies of Unlimited Success, Power, Beauty, or Ideal Love

The key word here is PREOCCUPIED. There can be something very healthy about aspiring to be successful, brilliant, beautiful, and giving ideal love; but when someone is preoccupied with it, there is often a tendency to be in it for oneself to the exclusion of another ... no matter the cost.

Entrepreneurs need to be careful here. A healthy person is able to see the value of the next area of growth for their company and is able to understand that a particular experience, even if negative, may be helpful to the overall good of the company. A healthy entrepreneur is able to separate himself or herself and their identity from the company. An unhealthy person feels that whatever level of success he or she has experienced is never enough. As a result, this person is often unable to separate self from company. He or she will view all experiences in life as part of a power play and will often view their businesses as their "family" instead of their spouse and children. An inability to separate self from business or career is often a sign of narcissism.

Another place we see this second symptom is in the area of extra-marital affairs. In my book: The State of Affairs, I discussed the five most common types of affairs and how marriages can be potentially healed after an affair. In most cases of infidelity, the adulterer suffers from the concept of believing they have found ideal love in their affair. They hang on to that thought to help rationalize the choice that oftentimes hurts others in their family. In extreme cases of an unfulfilling or abusive marriage one may be able to rationalize or at least understand the reason for an affair. More often than not, however, those in an affair idealize the relationship in the affair versus their marriage relationship. Frequently, the hope for an "ideal"relationship, represented by an illicit affair, is more attractive than the reality of a "real" relationship, represented by a marriage relationship.

Also included in this second symptom are folks that are driven toward physical perfection, a compulsive drive for outward physical perfection. Again, it is healthy to strive to be in shape and to care for oneself. A narcissist often takes this normal, healthy impulse to an extreme; a striving for outward appearance that trumps all else in their life. Often this striving prevents the narcissist from having balance in relationships, vocation and academics.

3. Belief that he or she is "Special" or Unique and can only be Understood by, or should Associate with, other Special or High-Status People (or Institutions).

Narcissists often believe that they are "special" or unique relative to other people and can only be understood by other, similar people; they "get it" while you or I don't. Whether it was my own experience in high school or seeing all the groups in the community where my daughters have been raised, or different faith communities or neighborhoods, there is usually a group of boys/men or girls/women who think they are "it" and nobody else really gets it. This is more than just exclusivity or cliquiness. Some members of these groups evolve into controlling or narcissistic people in their dance as an adult.

One of the things that I have observed from working with controllers or narcissistic types is that they often haven't evolved past adolescent egocentrism. The "us versus them" group mentality that I just mentioned is very common in adolescents in elementary, middle and high-school. Healthy people grow out of this as they move into more relativistic and pragmatic thinking as an adult. Healthy adults understand that while their group of friends may be "great," other groups are awesome as well, even if they are different than us. Narcissistic types don't evolve beyond this adolescent type of thinking. They stay stuck...a form of arrested development if you will.

4. Requires Excessive Admiration

Most people enjoy being admired, but narcissists REQUIRE it. I remember working with a couple. We will call them Joe and Sally. In their marriage, Joe was the co-dependent and Sally was controlling and moderately narcissistic. Sally needed to be acknowledged for what she did, this need trumped everything else. Although Joe was a bit more quiet, he tended to be generally positive in his words toward Sally. When Joe and Sally generally affirmed each other and avoided conflict, they got along just fine. When Joe voiced a concern about something that Sally said, however, Sally became enraged. Sally would then hang on to the one difficult thing that Joe said, ignoring all of the loving and positive things that he had said. Her reaction to what was not truly criticism but actually only a mild lack of admiration was entirely out of proportion to the input stimulus.

Recall that narcissists, especially those who grew up in shame, often feel that disagreement equals attack. The flip side of a narcissist's excessive need for admiration is an equally powerful fear of rejection, lack of attachment and shame. This often manifests as an irrational response - often a violent over-reaction - to a perceived lack of respect.

I remember working with another couple, Libby and John. John worked for his father. After 20 years of marriage, John discovered that Libby was having an affair. Naturally, he was devastated.
During personal therapy, he was talking about work when he related a story about landing the biggest account that his dad's company had ever acquired. When he excitedly told his dad about this achievement, his dad dismissed the achievement as nothing at all. John realized that he felt as if he was not acknowledged or loved by his dad. This feeling, in turn, caused him to seek excessive, and constant, affirmation from his spouse. In this case, John's life experience created an excessive neediness, a demand for affirmation that his spouse could not satisfy. The result is that Libby did not have the freedom to express herself in their marriage; his need for affirmation lead directly to an affair.

As discussed more fully in the pages to come, in some family systems, either the mom or dad may have this narcissistic trait. The child learns not to cross this parent. This feeling typically puts the child in a codependent framework, which will be discussed more fully in a later chapter of this book. Again they REQUIRE excessive admiration which often shows itself as being hypersensitive to any disagreements.

5. A Sense of Entitlement

Often, the narcissist will have a sense of entitlement, ie, unreasonable expectations of especially favorable treatment or automatic compliance with his or her expectations. We discussed earlier that one of the origins of narcissism can be growing up with an entitlement type of mentality.

6. Is Interpersonally Exploitative ie: takes Advantage of Others to Achieve his or her own ends.

Are all narcissists sociopaths? I believe, no. Are all sociopaths narcissistic … yes! So, not all narcissistic types have to get their own way to the point where they wake up each day intending to manipulate others. But, at the end of the day, most narcissists will do what they need to do to get their own way, including exploiting another. One of the ways this happens in the dance of narcissism and codependency is that the codependent ends up being too passive. The narcissist's spouse and children end up giving in, thus perpetuating a cycle of exploitation and manipulation. This part of the dance will be addressed in greater depth later in the book.

7. A Lack of Empathy

I remember that when one of our three daughters didn't make the high school top choir, I experienced a bit of this entitlement culture. We knew that our daughter was disappointed and, of course, we were sad for her. But, life goes on. As we were processing this experience, I received a few calls from other parents in the community who had heard that our daughter didn't make the top choir. They strongly encouraged me to call the choir director and to demand that he reconsider because our daughter had worked so hard and certainly deserved to make the choir. Although we resisted the urge to intervene on our daughter's behalf, the response of other parents showed such a strong sense of entitlement that it caused me to mention it here. The other parents clearly believed that no matter what the circumstance, they deserve to get what they want and if they don't, it's someone else's fault! While this reaction is not necessarily a sign of narcissism, it is a good example of the type of behavior exhibited by narcissists.

Another part of symptom five is the idea of automatic compliance to one's expectations. Typically, narcissistic types don't make requests, they make demands and expect immediate compliance. One of the ways I have seen this play out in relationships is when a young couple is trying to set up their own traditions for their children during the holidays. Sometimes the couple adjusts their plans based on the parent that would be MOST upset if they don't show up as usual on that holiday at the time the gathering has always been over the years. The most demanding parent of the system usually creates a compliant son/daughter. A more reasonable parent would be understanding of the couple's desire to start their own traditions and would be happy to have them at their house when it works, or at least would not shame them if it didn't work out on that day. The narcissistic parent, however, is rarely able to apply such nuanced discernment. The narcissist makes demands, not requests.

Another example of the narcissist's demand for automatic compliance plays out in handling disagreement. Often, the narcissist cannot handle a dating partner, spouse, parent, or child expressing disagreement with the narcissist's point of view. While it is common for one to be disappointed when someone disagrees with one's viewpoint, the narcissist is unable to separate this disappointment from a sense of betrayal.

Of all of the nine symptoms, this one is the most pervasive in narcissism. This one is felt most in couples and families that have a narcissist in the system. The inability to be empathetic, the inability to see and understand what the other person thinks and feels, cuts through significant relationships and automatically is a game changer. Unfortunately, this symptom is often times minimized or explained away by the codependent. Often, this most divisive characteristic is not addressed unless and until the codependent begins working on the relationship; an event that sometimes never occurs.

The concept of empathy is a powerful one. The inability or unwillingness to have this trait shows itself most when hurt is shown through words and actions in conflicts. The narcissist not only demands being right, they also have the unwillingness to confess when they've done wrong to their partner, spouse, child, or friend. The lack of being able to authentically say "I'm sorry" and mean it, drains the strength out of a relationship - big time.

6

8. Envious of Others and Believes Others are Envious of him or her.

Most people are guilty of envy at times. Many of us are envious of the love another couple has or how "perfect" their kids are. We can be envious of others' success, financially and physically. Envy of others is normal, at least when confined to reasonable levels. But what about the idea that we believe that others are envious of us? That requires a great deal of time and self-absorption. One of the characteristics of clinical narcissism is being so self-absorbed that others must not only think about him or her constantly, but actually envy him or her. Again, such self-absorption is relatively common among adolescents, but very rare among adults. If only a narcissist knew how this comes off to others!

9. Arrogant or Haughty Behavior and Attitudes

The last of the nine symptoms probably goes without saying, if one believes that he or she is better than everyone else, an arrogant attitude almost surely follows. Not all confidence is narcissistic, of course. We know that many times arrogance is not based in confidence, but instead is often rooted in deep insecurity. When someone is truly confident in who they are or what they believe, they don't need to win every argument, or have the last word in every conversation. True confidence often manifests itself as humility rather than arrogance.

I remember working with a couple whose oldest daughter married a narcissist. It was crushing to them and they were receiving help to try to learn how to deal with a difficult situation. Their son-in-law was a know-it-all, regardless of the topic; arrogant and belittling to those around him. What was most painful, however, was to watch his arrogance and condescension toward their daughter. While they earnestly desired to help their daughter break this cycle, those outside of the dance of narcissism often have to merely observe and support their family members caught in this cycle.

Narcissism, nature or nurture? The answer is yes, it is both! We have briefly discussed the basic environmental factors (nurture) that can potentially set the table for narcissism: factors like parental neglect, abandonment, and shame. A lack of attachment to an adult makes the child vulnerable to controlling his/her environment and bullying other people. This also promotes a lack of empathy which, in turn, causes one to obsessively focus on oneself. We have also discussed the environmental factor of entitlement and how growing up blaming everyone else for one's own limitations contributes to a sense of rage and control. The truth is that nurture often directly contributes, and may even cause, narcissistic tendencies.

What about nature? There are a potential innate, genetic, characteristics that can be contributing factors for narcissism. I will discuss a few of them:

1. Impulsivity. Some people do things, then they think. Impulsivity usually involves pleasure seeking and a lack of awareness of, or concern for, the consequences of one's actions. Impulsivity is often a genetically transmitted trait. If one has a predisposition toward impulsivity, and is also in an environment that does not appropriately help the person channel or direct their impulses into healthy choices, this person can become demanding, prideful, and arrogant.

2. Compulsivity. Some people are born with a need for order. I am constantly dealing with parents who say "my one child is a neat freak and my other one's room looks like a hurricane hit it and we've raised them both the same way!" Compulsivity typically has its roots in anxiety, which in turn is often caused by repressed fear. If a child's innate compulsive tendencies aren't harnessed or redirected in a healthy direction, they can sometimes develop a more severe condition like Obsessive-Compulsive disorder (OCD). OCD basically means that ones obsessive thoughts lead to compulsive behaviors. Folks that battle compulsivity can become narcissistic if they are not careful since things always need to be a certain way. When not appropriately directed, OCD tendencies can create rigid and inflexible people, very strong predictors of narcissistic tendencies.

As discussed above, neither impulsivity nor compulsivity automatically lead to narcissistic tendencies. Rather, this natural tendency requires proper nurture to avoid difficulties later in life. If a child is born with one or both of these tendencies (nature), it is important that the parent(s) steer those traits into healthy avenues (nurture).

3. Anxiety. There are several anxiety disorders which have a genetic cause. The most common one is generalized anxiety disorder (GAD). If someone has this condition, or is vulnerable to worry biologically, they sometimes can exhibit the traits of GAD which include excessive worry, restlessness, and irritability.

I remember a situation where a friend had to stop playing tennis because his spouse was worried that their 10 year old son who was biking two blocks to see him play might not get there safely. This friend was frustrated, but stopped playing tennis to make sure that his son was safe on his bike. The excessive worry of his spouse controlled the situation. Often untreated anxiety can create a controlling person who can eventually exhibit several narcissistic symptoms. As with many symptoms of narcissism, this is driven by fear of that which one cannot control.

4. Bipolar disorder. If someone has a genetic predisposition to bipolar, and they actually develop the illness, this often times has many characteristics of narcissism with it as well. In a manic episode, grandiosity and reckless behavior are the norm. In bipolar depression, the level of passivity and withdrawal can be severe and appear to be unending.

5. ADHD. Impulsivity, Hyperactivity , and Distractibility are the general headlines of this illness. If there is a genetic predisposition to these issues and it develops, often times narcissistic tendencies either come with it, or are developed from the same causes. Again, impulsivity brings forth excessive pleasure seeking, blurting out information and getting what one wants; while hyperactivity can produce an individual whose actions seem like they are all about themselves, and distractibility/inattentiveness often times comes off as disinterest, a lack of quality time and as if that person doesn't care.

With these and other potential mental health illnesses, sometimes narcissism is a co-morbid condition. My own belief about nature/nurture is that genetics certainly matter...they can indicate a predisposition to certain narcissistic tendencies. With appropriate environmental guidance, and especially if the parent(s) are healthily self-aware, however, the nurture piece can help rein in nature issues and sometimes even redirect them into healthy avenues!

Lastly, remember that a diagnosis of Narcissistic Personality Disorder requires a finding of at least five of these traits. Remember, too, that narcissism is a continuum; the more traits exhibited by the person, the more pronounced will the narcissistic tendency be. It is very important not to rush to judgment based upon one or two of these symptoms. A person can exhibit one or two of the nine symptoms of narcissistic personality disorder and have only mild narcissistic tendencies. It is important to understand that having a controlling tendency doesn't mean the person is a full blown narcissist, but the controlling tendencies can make someone vulnerable to the condition if it is not addressed or acknowledged.

CHAPTER 2

CODEPENDENCY...THE ULTIMATE PEOPLE-PLEASING LIFE

Co-dependency has been a buzz-word in clinical circles for a long time. I would like to go over the seven symptoms that I have generally seen in codependents.

1. Taking on the other person's feelings

One of the main struggles for a co-dependent is that they tend to measure their own actions based upon how they anticipate another person will react. In other words, they have conversations with themselves about whether what they feel, think, or want to say has any merit, based mostly on how the other person is going to react.

For example, I was working with a woman, we will call her Lynne, who was 12 years into marriage. She felt that she was building resentment toward her spouse and she wasn't liking the way she was feeling. She reported that she would constantly be assessing her spouse's feelings before she would say or do anything. She had grown, for lack of a better phrase, too other-centered!

How did this start for her? Well, as is often the case, this was a pattern she brought into the marriage. Her father was extremely moody, controlling, and harsh. She would do whatever she could to try to anticipate this response before she would speak. She never wanted to upset him because there would be hell to pay ... the pattern of being so other centered started early for her and continued throughout her upbringing. As this book will suggest, Lynne's mother played the role of a codependent and allowed her father to treat Lynne and her three brothers this way.

With her upbringing plus 12 years of marriage to practice, Lynne was now a pro co-dependent. Now, however, she was growing weary of it and had finally realized the key truth that the co-dependent needs to learn: The controller/narcissistic type will never change as long as I put up with their controlling behavior.

As an aside, taking on other's feelings not only affects one's emotions. When we take on other's feelings, we are doubling our own emotional response, often overwhelming our body's defense mechanisms. As Lynne learned, this, in turn, can cause our body to experience physical symptoms such as panic and stress. Our body only has room for one set of emotions, our own!

2. Adapting to the other person's moods

This symptom is close to the first one I explained. As the co-dependent becomes proficient at reading their spouse's, partner's feelings, they also learn how to adjust themselves based on whatever mood the other person is having. I call this being "outside-in" where you end up being defined by other's thoughts, feelings, moods, choices, and begin to adjust your own to meet those. By contrast, an "inside-out" person would be defined by your own thoughts, feelings, and choices, which are brought from inside the person out into the world. Because the controlling, potentially narcissistic, spouse is so difficult to live with, the co-dependent often defaults into trying to keep the peace by playing dodgeball with their spouse or loved ones moods - anything to keep the mood manageable.

One of the biggest challenges of a co-dependent's adaptation to a controlling person's moods is that the person they spend most of their time adapting to is the most unhealthy person in their universe. They become drawn to that sibling, child, parent, spouse that is the most neurotic or narcissistic because they are the one with the most undesirable mood most of the time. This is the very reason why the co-dependent can get so tired, hurt, angry, resentful, and victimized.

3. Pacifying to avoid conflicts

Co-dependents don't necessarily always come from a difficult upbringing. Let's visit with Josie and Ken. Ken's upbringing was reasonably calm. His parents were more internal in general. They would have conflicts but neither person would get overly demanding or unreasonable with each other or with Ken and his two siblings (one male, one female). So Ken was used to conflicts, but he was also used to having them handled reasonably. Enter

Josie. Josie's mom was a yeller. She also had a need to be right and would get right into your face and tell you so until you acquiesced to her view. Josie was the oldest of three daughters. So...now that Ken and Josie have been married for a year or two, a pattern was evolving. When Josie would get upset, she would follow her mother's lead and rage at Ken. Ken didn't know what to make of it. It didn't always happen, but enough so that it became the norm when they would have a conflict. Ken began to realize that the "best" way to deal with this would be to do what he could, whenever he could, to AVOID any disagreement with Josie. Josie was "fine" when there wasn't a disagreement. So in order to AVOID a conflict, Ken would pacify. He would agree at all costs. No matter what. Ken thought...."why would I want to have a conflict anyway?" "Things aren't THAT bad...are they?" " My needs don't matter THAT much. It's better to be a peacekeeper versus a trouble starter"...or so he thought.

Another theme you will start to see in the book is that in situations that are similar to Ken and Josie's marriage and family, the Josies of the world don't think that there is anything wrong in their relationships; oh my are they wrong! So long as the Kens of the world continue to pacify to avoid conflicts, the "dance" of narcissism and co-dependency carries on without a hitch. I wish I had a dollar for every Josie that was in for counseling and would suggest that she/he was shocked that their spouse, child, etc was ready to leave or was extremely resentful. When we avoid the mess, we carry the mess.

4. Becoming Easily Controlled

The pacifying and adjusting in everyday life automatically creates a controlling, parent-child type of marriage/partnership dance. In seeking to avoid conflict, the co-dependent does not offer his or her perspective on a thought, feeling, decision, or choice. Over time, the co-dependent become resentful and develops a feeling of being controlled. The co-dependent would rather agree than create an unfair fight. As a result, the narcissist effectively gains powerful control over the co-dependent, control which is in a very real sense voluntarily ceded by the co-dependent.

Of course the controller doesn't see this at all. They feel things are great. They can talk to their spouse, children, however they want, because they know they can. Yes, the control not only occurs to the co-dependent spouse/partner; it bleeds down to the kids as well. For example, let's look at

LaTasha and Ali. In their dance, Ali is the controller/narcissist and LaTasha is the co-dependent. They have two children whom LaTasha has already "brainwashed" to avoid conflict with Ali just to keep the peace. So, in this family dance, Ali's control will continue and get stronger. There is no other "voice" in the family, just Ali's. His intimidating anger is a huge issue in this family, not only today, but in the generations to come. Because the kids are being coached to avoid conflict with their father, this unhealthy pattern will likely continue into their own romantic journeys as well if they are not careful to reverse the pattern.

One might say that by avoiding conflicts, LaTasha and Ali are ensuring "peace" in the house. While it is true that avoiding conflicts will temporarily ensure peace, in the long run, this false sense of peace is merely enforced by control. Control can create passivity, but passivity and avoidance can create a control dynamic as well. The almost certain end result of each of these interpersonal dynamics is conflict, either now or at some point in the future. People need to remember that peace is actually achieved through healthily mediated conflict!

5. Doesn't know self well

Typically, the co-dependent knows the other person's thoughts and feelings well. The co-dependent spends so much time and energy anticipating their spouse's feelings and potential reactions, they become quite aware of their controlling spouse. Often, however, they do not know themselves as well. They spend relatively less time being aware of their own thoughts, feelings, and needs, meaning that they are not in touch with themselves.

For example, let's focus on a family with one controlling parent and another co-dependent parent along with three sons. In that system, it is likely that unless the co-dependent spouse confronts and asserts their needs, one of the kids, typically the middle child, will become acutely aware of how to avoid conflicts with the controlling parent and sibling(s). This particular child will be developing the "outside-in" way of life that I explained earlier and rarely is aware of or asserts their own needs and feelings. This pattern becomes very prominent in their life and is likely to follow them into their most significant friendships and romantic relationships.

This person's own feelings and thoughts are just not well developed. They get comfortable with assessing others versus knowing self. Again, this isn't the worst issue in the world, but it often leads to stress and other co-dependent choices in their life. The minimization of self might sound initially like a positive thing, too much self can be a problem; but the truth is that a healthy, loving view of self allows someone to love others well, create good boundaries, and have reasonable dialogues about life issues as they arise. The identity of the co-dependent becomes shaped by how others view them and react to them. Obviously, awareness of others can be very good, it only becomes an issue when the co-dependent lacks confidence to assert their own voice.

6. Not having a voice in the relationship

This lack of a voice in their relationship(s) is fully a result of not knowing what to say, or actually being concerned that what they might say is "wrong." I often advise clients to lovingly confront their spouse with their concern and feelings. I am often told that this confrontation didn't go "well." When I ask for more details, the client frequently explains that their spouse "reacted in a harsh way, so I must have confronted them in the 'wrong' way." This is a common reaction of a co-dependent. The truth most often is that the co-dependent was able to have his or her voice heard, but the narcissist disagreed. I explain to clients that, in this situation, the truth is out and the table is set for further conversations. Having a voice in the relationship is a key antidote for the co-dependent that we will be discussing later in the book. The alternative to having a voice is not having a voice at all! Having a voice doesn't mean winning a fight or getting the last word in; it just means being open and honest about the great things and the difficult things.

7. May endure abuse or poor treatment

The scariest part of co-dependency is that the co-dependent endures. I'm often asked, "why am I drawn to a controlling, potentially abusive and narcissistic person." I usually tell that client that I don't think they went out looking for a harsh, controlling person at all. The issue is often that once that type of behavior shows itself, the co-dependent blames himself or herself for the narcissist's behavior. The co-dependent frequently convinces themselves that they either "deserve" this reaction or that they are doing something to cause the behavior. After all, the controlling person isn't ALWAYS controlling;

he or she can be funny, charming, loving, helpful, and enjoyable sometimes. Because the co-dependent feels blame for the behavior, it can set them up to endure it. The reactions of control under stress, the need to be right, getting the last word in and a lack of empathy are patterns that need to be ADDRESSED not ENDURED! Sadly, most often the co-dependent will endure, not address.

The other issue about enduring is that the co-dependent might know why their controlling/narcissistic parent, spouse, adult child, etc ... is acting the way they are. They may know that they have been through a trauma, or have had a difficult upbringing. They may know that the reason they overreact or get intimidating is "understandable" for how they grew up or how they were treated in their last relationship. BUT, by the co-dependent enduring vs. addressing, the controlling person never gets better, they never heal ... in fact, they usually get worse. So, the co-dependent isn't doing anyone any favors by enduring this type of treatment. Not themselves, not their children, and not their controlling/narcissistic spouse.

CHAPTER 3

THE DANCE

There are some key features that develop early on in the dance. In this chapter I will discuss some of these important features that the couple and family need to consider in order to avoid falling into unhealthy patterns.

Controllers/Narcissists win the fights ... Pleasers/Codependents acquiesce

Early on in the dance of a couple or family's journey together there can be long periods where there are very few conflicts. During periods of few or no conflicts it is difficult to understand or identify the dance. Of course, even during good times narcissistic types will want things to go a certain way and the codependent will go along. So, in a sense, the pattern is already starting but is not as noticeable. The dance gets a bit more visble early on when stress develops. One of the ways that this part of the dance becomes noticeable is when an incident happens between the couple or in the family system. Often times fights early on in the dance occur over whether to do something with each other's friends or not; or in the area of spending money. Regardless of the conflict or stressor, the controller will make demands to get his or her own way and the codependent starts their long journey of acquiescing to the controller's demands. It is important to note that at this point the narcissist is clear in their mind that there is nothing wrong, and the codependent is clear that they were frustrated by that interaction. One key missing element in this interaction is the co-dependent's ability to be honest about what they are feeling. Let me be clear here....the codependent's inability to be honest is as unhealthy as the controller's need to be right.

Let's take an example of Bob and Kathy. Bob grew up in a home with a father who was very narcissistic, and his mother was extremely codependent. Bob learned early on that disagreeing with his father was not worth it and he was better off going along with his father's demands. This pattern for Bob continued throughout his upbringing and into joining his father's business. Kathy, on the other hand, grew up in a home where her father was more quiet and allowed Kathy to have her own voice. Kathy's mother tended to be more insistent on her own way, so Kathy learned this pattern as well. So as we review the two dances that Bob and Kathy came from we see that in Bob's case there was a clear controller/narcissistic type and codependent, while in Kathy's dance it could be viewed that mom had some controlling tendencies and dad was more passive. So now that Bob and Kathy became married and started their dance, we see both of them continuing the patterns that they learned. Kathy would initiate her feelings about an issue or a situation, and Bob, generally whether he agreed or not, would go along. At work, Bob was also getting more and more responsibilities as his father was aging so Bob started to develop his voice at work a bit. Bob continued to be frustrated with acquiescing to his father's choices at work, and also his ongoing acquiescence with his wife Kathy at home. Bob also saw that his four children were doing quite well. They saw a nurturing father along with the mother who had her voice. Often this recipe lends itself well to raising healthy children. The issue that brought Bob and Kathy into counseling, however, was that Bob clearly was becoming more and more unhappy with acquiescing to both his father and his wife. Bob started to share his frustrations with both people. He learned from the counseling how to have a healthy "come to Jesus talk" with his father. Over time Bob became more comfortable with having his voice heard with his father at work, due to the fact that he was gaining responsibility and was starting to take over the company. In his marriage with Kathy, however, he was continuing to do what he knew would make Kathy happy. In and of itself, that can be a good thing to offer in marriage to one's spouse or partner. But the codependent is doing so in a way which is not honest about their own feelings and views. Thus, resentment builds, and the codependent starts to distance themselves from their spouse.

Controller/Narcissists instruct & parent...Codependents listen & follow

Another part of the dance that starts early on is that the controlling person, or a full-blown narcissist, starts to create a parent-child type of relationship. This part of the dance looks clearly like a parent-child relationship. As the couple is living day to day, the narcissist makes the choices for them while the codependent listens and follows instructions. The controlling or narcissistic person offers advice unsolicited, to their spouse or partner regardless of the topic being discussed. Narcissists often can come off like "know it alls". Friends of this particular couple often see the parent-child dilemma developing and will find themselves saying: "why does he/she let him/her treat him/her like that?" Let's take the example of Tyshel and Amber. Tyshel grew up with a dominant father in an extremely passive-avoidant mother. While Amber grew up with a mother who was nurturing and supportive and an absent father who had left the home when Amber was a child. As Tyshel and Amber started their dance, Tyshel's moods controlled the home. He would give Amber an allowance for the money she could spend. He would suggest who she should and who she shouldn't spend time with in her friendships. He would say what he would be doing that night with his friends regardless

18

of Amber's needs. Amber's friends could not believe that she was putting up with this from Tyshel. They would confront her about this and Amber would suggest that it wasn't that bad. Amber learned early on that disappointing Tyshel led to him having intense reactions just as he experienced from his father when he tried to disagree with him. Amber sorted out her options and felt that it made more sense to let herself be with a man who she knew loved her, partially because she had no male role model in her own life growing up, versus having her own voice with Tyshel in developing an adult to adult relationship versus the parent-child. Again I would suggest that the codependents' inability to be honest and create their own voice of truth is a key component in this unhealthy part of the dance continuing. Of course, the narcissist's demands as well as intimidating and manipulative style of control make it extremely difficult for the codependent to develop their own identity and to be confident in that.

Controllers/Narcissists don't know anything is wrong...Codependents build resentment

As we have discussed with both Bob and Kathy and Tysel and Amber it is clear that the controllers in both stories did not think there was anything wrong, while the codependents were slowly becoming frustrated and building their resentment bank accounts. This part of the dance starts early and continues all the way to the next section of the book which will talk about what eventually happens in the dance. One of the most common statements I will receive from a controlling\narcissistic person is that they didn't realize anything was wrong in their marriage or partnership. One of the most common statements I will receive from a codependent person is that they have become resentful and can never see themselves being close to the controller again.

From the outside looking in, we might say why in the world wouldn't the narcissists see what is wrong? Well, as we have discussed in Chapter 1 with the typical narcissistic type we see that one of their main struggles is a lack of empathy. They don't receive a response back from their codependent spouse or partner that there is anything wrong and, due to their lack of empathy, they cannot believe that there would be anything wrong. As such, the controller continues to believe that everything is fine. Later in the book I will discuss the key antidotes to changing the dance and changing some of the most common generational patterns that there are in family systems.

From the outside looking in, we might also say why in the world wouldn't the codependent say that they are building resentment and develop their voice? As we learned from the symptomatology of codependency in Chapter 2, codependents very early on lack any sense of self and spend most of their time trying to either avoid conflict, interpret their partner's feelings or do what needs to be done in order for things to be okay. Again, for the codependent, conflicts feel bad and wrong. Conflicts don't end up going well. I often hear from codependents that they would rather take the hit and slowly build resentment versus causing fights and have the children experience conflict.

This sense that the controller doesn't know that there is anything wrong while the codependent is building resentment starts from the very first day of their partnership or marriage and continues until the codependent speaks up. Unfortunately, most of the time the codependent doesn't speak up for at least 10 to 20 years into the partnership or marriage. And sometimes they never speak up ... they just endure.

Entitlement

One of the key features to recognizing the dance is the narcissist's sense of entitlement. As I mentioned in chapter 1, whether it is from abandonment and rejection from a primary caregiver or always getting what they want, the controller regularly acts entitled. This feature kicks the codependent into their gear of compliance. Again, the option of challenging this sense of entitlement seems daunting to the codependent. They would rather avoid versus confront. Another component of the codependent's resentment bank account however is their view that their spouse or partner's sense of entitlement is outrageous. They can't believe their spouse or partner would actually act that way! The codependent often finds themselves saying: "I would never do that or say something like that." "If I said that to him/her, there would be hell to pay." "This sense of entitlement doesn't seem fair." Now, instead of saying these statements to the narcissist/controller, they keep it to themselves and the entitlement reign continues.

Let's look at the case of William and Sarah. William is the narcissist/controller and Sarah is the codependent. William was caught by Sarah in his second affair. His first affair occurred just two years into his marriage with Sarah. He ended that affair but was not remorseful. He felt entitled to the affair due to Sarah's lack of sexual companionship with him. Sarah ended up resuming her sexual relationship with her husband after his first affair in order to keep him in the marriage. During counseling, we found that Sarah was withholding her sexual feelings due to his commanding and controlling nature. So after several years of having sex regularly in the marriage against her will, Sarah started to withdraw from William sexually. This is when William started his second affair. Like the first, he felt entitled to continue the affair. Now, after Sarah caught him in his second affair, she started to be honest about why, throughout the course of their marriage, she would withdraw sexually. William couldn't believe what he was hearing. He did not view himself as demanding or controlling. He felt as if he was treating her just like all of his employees at the business he owned! The case of William and Sarah is very common in our society today. Often the narcissist's sense of entitlement and superiority leads to a double life. It is likely the William and Sarah's marriage will not get better and Sarah will probably leave the relationship. By being honest about her feelings, however, Sarah may be able to alleviate her resentment and learn to protect herself. Although William will probably never recognize his broken nature and how his lack of empathy has contributed to his struggles, at least he now actually knows how his spouse feels. Again, just like the other parts of the dance discussed so far a key element in learning to dance more effectively is the codependent's ability to be honest.

Controllers/Narcissists look for what is wrong with their spouse ... Pleasers/Codependents tend to glamorize their spouse

Consistent with the earlier section of the dance chapter, we discussed the idea that narcissists tend to instruct and parent their spouse, the narcissist's lack of empathy makes it virtually impossible for them to see the good in their spouse. They tend to look for what's wrong and they will let their spouse know what's wrong. By staying on this offensive type of process, the narcissist gains and maintains control. The codependent's reaction to this through their own deep sense of denial and inferiority, is to actually overcompensate for this issue by glamorizing their spouse. They will be the one that always says: "Isn't he or she wonderful?!" Some observers of these statements may find it honorable that the codependent says this about their spouse but they will also be aware of how the narcissist cuts down their spouse. I have mentioned earlier in the chapter this comes off very discouraging to friends and loved ones.

The narcissist's criticism operates to control the spouse, keeping the codependent on the defensive. They are always looking for a chance to get approval from this narcissistic spouse. The codependent tells themselves: "If I can just be nice enough then I might get a compliment," or " if I'm nice enough then maybe they will not cut me down in front of our friends," or, " if I affirm him or her enough in front of our friends then maybe they will be in a good mood that evening when we get home". This dynamic is a powerful one through the majority of the dance. The critical nature of the controller allows them to feel confident even though they are deeply insecure. It allows them to avoid being on the defense or being bullied like they often were by their most dominant parent. The other reason this feature of the dance continues is that it is rare that a friend of the narcissist would confront him or her about how they criticize their spouse or partner. Often the narcissist's best friend or friends find themselves being codependent as well. Likewise the codependent's friend or friends find themselves wanting to avoid telling their own feelings to their codependent friend because they might feel like he or she has enough on their plate. While it certainly isn't up to the spouses' friends to cure their dance it can be powerful when neither the narcissist's friends confronts him or her about how critical they are and how disgusting that is, or the codependent's friends say how difficult it is for them to watch him or her being treated so poorly. When the friends of the couple stand up and talk about this issue one-on-one, you can either provide some clarity or be a vehicle to the changing of the friendship.

Controllers/Narcissists tend to get more controlling …
Pleasers/Codependents tend to get more passive

Another interesting feature in the dance of narcissism and codependency is that sometimes a couple does not start out that way. Once in a while a mildly controlling and mildly passive couple starts out that way. But even in these particular cases the tendency to control continues and the tendency to be passive continues. Even with that mild dynamic, more often than not, the controlling person can develop a narcissistic trait or two and the passive person can develop some codependent traits. I have worked with many couples where a particular spouse has a mild anxiety disorder. In the case of Bianca and Collin, Bianca's anxiety disorder caused her to have excessive worry and to occasionally over protect her children. This worry was noted and noticed by her spouse. Instead of her spouse confronting her about the worry and suggesting to her that he was concerned about it, he would, through his passivity, try to circumvent the choices the couple made in order to prevent her from worrying. When she would overprotect the children, he would agree in order to help stop her worry. Colin thought that by helping her worry less, her anxiety would decrease. But actually it works in reverse. The worrier will always worry about something. Often in the marriage relationship a worrier can become controlling. If the passive spouse does not assert that he or she is not worried about a particular situation that their spouse is worried about and offers their own view, the worry will prevail. Obviously, the majority of people battling an anxiety disorder do not develop several narcissistic traits, but some do. The ones that do usually marry a passive person who's worry and passivity gets worse.

The majority of the time, this dance starts with people who exhibit several narcissistic traits and several codependent traits. As we learned from earlier sections of this chapter, the evolution of the dance gets worse versus better. The day to day demanding non-empathetic, arrogant and entitled feelings of the controller will trump any view the codependent has. As we mentioned earlier, acquiescence from the codependent starts early so that type of behavioral pattern continues and accelerates through the course of the marriage.

Up to this point the majority of what I have discussed with the dance involves a couple. I would now like to shift to the impact of the dance on the children involved in that family system.

CHAPTER 4

THE DANCE & ITS IMPACT ON THE CHILDREN

I was talking with a couple I knew well recently when they mentioned that there seems to be an increase in mental health issues in society. I agreed with this premise, but also mentioned to them that one growing area of interest in the field of mental health is more protective factors.

Protective factors allow mental health issues to be addressed earlier in people's stories. One of the greatest protective factors there is in our society is for parents to "get it." In other words, if we have a family where one person has untreated bipolar disorder along with narcissistic symptoms and they marry someone who falls into a codependent framework, then it is likely that the bipolar features will carry down to one or more of the children. With that in mind we see the dance occurring and observing the children choosing between becoming naturally more narcissistic and controlling or becoming codependent and pleasing themselves.

The dance has a particularly acute impact upon children. As we discovered earlier, the better parents understand and address their own personal dance, the greater the likelihood we have to be able to resolve and create more protective factors to allow children to avoid the negative impacts of the dance.

REBELLIOUS or COMPLIANT

The first impact that I have seen in my practice on children regarding the dance of narcissistic tendencies is that the child or children either become more rebellious or more compliant with the controlling/narcissistic type parent. Recalling from an earlier chapter on narcissism, the controller needs to be right and to "win." The narcissist creates an environment where it is not safe for others to express their opinions. The child growing up in this type of domineering environment will frequently develop a pleaser/codependent personality framework. The child learns early to mimic the pleaser/codependent parent by avoiding saying or doing things that will set off the controlling/narcissistic type parent.

The child therefore has to have discussions with him or herself because the narcissistic and codependent parents do not create a framework where the child can create a healthy dialogue with the parents. Instead, the child may create an

23

internal dialogue, not shared with the parents, which is safe. The child does not feel free to share his or her own feelings in a way that makes him or her feel safe. The child feels stuck between a narcissistic parent and a codependent parent. And thus, the dance continues.

Sometimes the child does not develop a codependent framework but instead becomes very agitated, very irritable, very defiant. This child may tend to see very early on the narcissistic parent's hypocrisy. The controlling narcissistic type parent essentially teaches the child to "do as I say, not as I do."

Some children in this environment will adopt a less passive and more direct conversational style. Perhaps the child has more impulsivity in their makeup or perhaps they feel more comfortable simply saying what is on their minds more quickly because they have that type of impulsivity. The child may tend to blurt out whatever comes to mind rather than being careful about what they say. It is more likely that this type of child will develop a rebellious type of framework in that family system.

What we are noticing so far is that the dance often creates a system where the child or children will choose between two unhealthy options; A need to be right or a need to be liked. Often, the child does not learn how to reach a healthy balance between between speaking the truth and having empathy.

Let's discuss an example of how this rebellion or compliance to a controlling or narcissistic type parent plays itself out. Consider the story of Robert and Susan. Robert has a mildly narcissistic personality style. Mild in the sense that he has some awareness that he tends to be arrogant. His wife Susan has been some individual therapy to help her create some healthy boundaries for the relationship that she finds herself in. Robert and Susan have three children. The oldest is Elizabeth. The second born is Joy, and the youngest is Davis.

The tendency that I have noticed in these types of stories is that when the firstborn is of the opposite sex from the controlling/narcissistic type parent they tend toward a more pleaser/codependent framework. The firstborn is often hard working, conscientious and overachieving. These children are often driven by a desire to please the controlling/narcissistic type parent and can themselves often be bossy and parental.

In this particular case, Robert's narcissistic edges were recognized by both Elizabeth and Joy. Elizabeth found herself being more pleaser based, wanting to receive her father's approval and wanting Robert to acknowledge her perfectionism. Because of his narcissistic tendencies and limited insights into others, however, Robert rarely gave Elizabeth the acknowledgement that she needed.

The second born, Joy, bounces off Elizabeth in this story and ends up being more frustrated with how her father treats her mother. Due to this framework, Joy gets into more arguments with her father. This might not seem like a typical middle child, but Joy has learned from Elizabeth and has rejected the codependent framework. Like many middle children, Joy has been watching her siblings, has closely watched the dance and does not like what she sees. Joy starts to confront her father about how he is treating the family. As a narcissist, Robert, of course, has to win the fight with his daughter.

As a codependent, Susan consoles Joy about how Robert has treated her. Joy will have then have arguments with Susan about why she doesn't stand up for herself. So far you've noticed that the oldest has taken on a more compliant framework while the middle child has developed a rebellious framework.

The third born, Davis, has a need to get what he wants as youngest children often tend to do. He is four years younger than Joy so he has also had separate time to look at this dance. He and his father have more fights. He has developed a more rebellious framework as well. The is a story where two of the three children are more rebellious and one is more compliant. There are many stories where this experience is reversed and more of the children end up being compliant. The key point is that when there is a narcissistic type parent in the home, the children unfortunately tend to evolve to one extreme or the other because they have seen no middle ground modeled.

FEELING SORRY or BEING ANGRY

The second impact that the dance has on the children is that the children tend to either feel sorry for or become angry with the codependent parent.   I referred to this a little bit with Joy earlier. She is getting frustrated with her mother because she perceives her to be weak and allowing herself to be treated badly. Susan tends to minimize the situation and tells Joy "it isn't that big of a deal." Because Susan has done some counseling, however, these words don't make sense to Susan either. Often in the codependent's desire to get better and to have a voice, the codependent still tries to protect the children from the narcissist. The codependent wants the children to have their own voice even if the codependent does not have a voice of his or her own.

The oldest child, Elizabeth, is tending to feel sorry for the mother. Elizabeth sees how the father is treating her and sees over time Susan's needs are not being met. Elizabeth, over time, is starting to see that her desire for approval of her father often goes unnoticed. Elizabeth experiences a growing frustration from this unmet need even though she remains compliant. This growing disconnect is then met with sorrow and a growing sense of compassion for her mother. So Elizabeth in the story is choosing to feel sorry for Susan rather than feeling anger towards her. This example shows how children may be impacted by the dance. Each of the children feels a need to take something on in response to the dance between their narcissistic father and their codependent mother.

When a child is exposed to those kinds of impulses, they are required to take on their parents' issues rather than to pursue their own story. Too early in their story they're having to decide that their own identity requires them to address issues that more properly belong to their parents. Dealing with these issues may make children feel overwhelmed and may develop into a type of toxic fumes which prevents normal development.

In this story Davis has a mixture of feelings for his family. He finds himself sometimes feeling sorry for his mother about the way his dad is treating her and sometimes feels angry that she is not sticking up for herself. He finds himself experiencing both extremes. He allows himself to communicate those feelings to Susan and is very frustrated that she allows dad to treat her that way. Davis does not understand either why his father is so harsh or why his mother is so passive. One of the biggest things I tell couples is that because of the dance of controlling versus pleasing tendencies they create in their home, they are only giving their children two choices: to become rebellious or to become compliant and passive. They are not teaching their child/children to develop a healthy balance of assertiveness and empathy.

IMITATE

The third and most long-term impact on the children is that the children tend to imitate one or the other parent in their own eventual adult relationships. It is likely that Elizabeth in this story will allow herself to be drawn toward, or endure, a partner who does not treat her well. She may be more vulnerable to realizing that no matter how hard she tries for perfectionism, it still does not achieve the approval that she is seeking. She also may tend to be more compliant believing that her partner's responses and attitudes are her fault. Because of her upbringing, she may not see that this life view is unhealthy. The theory with Elizabeth is that she may potentially recreate the story where she becomes the more codependent spouse like her mother Susan and may endure and marry someone like Robert.

In the case of Joy, we noticed that she has gotten more angry with her father and is frustrated with how he is treating her mother. As Joy develops in her adolescent and young adult life, she will perhaps be more vulnerable to saying that no one will treat her like her father treats her mother. In that way, Joy may become more vulnerable to controlling her relationships. The feeling that she is never right in family discussions may lead Joy to overcompensate by always needing to be right in her own relationships later in her story.

Finally, as we look at Davis, we expect that his need to be right as the last born coupled with his father's aggressive style, and then mixed with the anger and compassion he feels toward his mother will make for a very complicated experience as he considers his own life partner later in his story. In some of these types of cases, I have noticed that the male children are more vulnerable to being noncommittal, and often avoiding romantic relationships entirely. When there are conflicts in his own relationships, he will be less likely to be able to resolve these conflicts in a healthy manner. He has learned to either avoid or overreact to conflicts in his own story. Having experienced relational toxicity in his own upbringing, he may also be far less likely to risk the same in his own potential romantic relationships.

When I see a couple with children, I explain how the work they are doing on their own relationship is a gift to their children. When the more controlling parent can learn to think before speaking, increase empathy and draw out his or her spouse, the child learns to do the same. Likewise, when the codependent spouse learns to speak his or her own mind, to be assertive, to be okay with disagreement, the children are learning better balance. When both parents are doing this critical work on themselves and their own relationship, the gift that they have given to their children is profound and long lasting!

Chapter 5

What Eventually Happens

So far I've discussed the impact of narcissism and codependency on couples and families through the early part of their life story. As we have discussed, narcissists tend to instruct and parent while codependents tend to listen and follow. Narcissists tend to win the fights while codependents acquiesce. Narcissists often are not aware that there is anything wrong while codependents are painfully aware and build resentment. Controllers also feel a sense of entitlement and that there is something wrong with their codependent spouse as he or she becomes more and more withdrawn.

The codependent spouse, in turn, tends to glamorize their spouse despite obvious problems in their personality. Finally, a pattern that is starting to take shape in those early to middle years is where the controlling narcissistic person becomes more and more controlling while the codependent person becomes more and more passive. These developing issues lead us to ask what happens in later life. By the time the couple has been married for 15 or 20 years, on average, they reach a point where they settle into more of a midlife process. During the midlife years, whether it's triggered by children being out of the home or retirement or another change in life situations, I have noticed that three types of situations that tend to evolve.

The Codependent Gives in & Gives up

The first situation is what I have observed that happens most of the time. The codependent "gives in and gives up." What does this look like? Consider the case of Katrina, a very controlling spouse, and Michael, a very passive spouse. They have two daughters who are grown and on their own. Michael has seen that when he tries to lovingly confront his spouse about something in the marriage, he finds her to be intimidating, mean, and emotionally dysregulated. Because the narcissist has to win the fight, Michael has learned not to bother to engage, instead simply shutting down and no longer even bothering to stick up for himself. Michael starts to see Katrina confronting their daughters in ways that are harsher than he would. He has made a few attempts to confront her, but those attempts have been repulsed, at least in his mind.

Michael has concluded that it's just not worth it to confront Katrina and therefore has chosen to keep the peace.

Peacemakers are often people who pursue peace in difficult situations, while peacekeepers avoid the mess of confrontation and instead settle for a "peaceful" coexistence. By becoming a peace keeper, Michael has concluded that it is easier to give in and keep the peace than to fight to make the peace. Giving up is therefore easier for Michael and appears to be something that he can "handle" as he performs damage control with the children. The main reason that this is such a common result is that the controlling person doesn't think there's anything wrong. Often, the children of a controller are so emotionally controlled that the children act "perfectly" around him or her, hoping to avoid any outburst by the narcissist parent. As a result, when there are problems with the children, the narcissist assumes that it must be the fault of the codependent, continuing the dance of dysfunction. One additional reason that the narcissist is unaware of problems is the codependent spouse has given in and given up, choosing to minimize the issues and not identify or address any of the problems.

The Codependent Hits the Wall & has a Midlife Crisis

The second option that we see happen is the codependent "hits the wall" and has a midlife crisis. Take the situation of Terrance and Molly who married early in life. Molly was third of six children and tended to listen to her mother talk about how unhappy her marriage was. Molly became a classic pleaser by listening to her mother as she complained about her relationship with Molly's father. Molly was a great friend to others and was the person that people felt comfortable talking to. When she met Terrance in high school she enjoyed listening to Terrance, he set up the dates and would talk a lot. Terrance helped her with her homework and took care of her car. Terrance was always "helping" and "taking care of" Molly in high school. Terrence was available and she wanted to get out of the house, so they married early. The problem for Molly was that she was now continuing to listen, this time to Terrance instead of her mother. Like her mother had done, Terrance began to complain to Molly about all of his stress at work, with friends and what she was doing wrong in the marriage. Molly simply listened and endured, just as she had done growing up with her mother. Molly still had her friendships from high school and college and was listening to their issues and trying to be helpful to them as well. Molly would still get weekly phone calls and daily texts from her mother and would listen to her complaints. Molly and Terrance had three children. Molly, as a good codependent, became responsible and did 90% of the work at home. While their children were young, Molly stayed home and raised the children while Terrance worked outside the home. When the children entered high school, Molly went back to work and used her degree to do very well working in human resources with a local company. Molly continued to move up in the company and was given promotions and new opportunities. After about 10 years with the company she found herself feeling very comfortable at work and met a coworker named William. William actually asked her how she was doing and expressed interest in who she was. Molly began to find her emotional needs being met by William. Over time, Molly and William became closer as they worked on projects. They ended up traveling together for work projects and eventually began an intimate relationship. William encouraged Molly to work on her marriage relationship and Molly began having extreme feelings of guilt. Molly found herself in a full-blown midlife crisis: she loved her children but found that she no longer loved her husband. Just as happened with Molly and Terrance, the codependent often hits the wall and has a midlife crisis.

Narcissistic/controller type people's capacity to love is not as great as their need to be loved. Terrance's inability to love his spouse well made her vulnerable to receive care from another who could better respond to her needs. To be sure, Molly is at fault here for not speaking out to Terrance earlier about her needs, for not creating healthy boundaries with her mother and with Terrance. Often, however, both the narcissist and codependent unintentionally contribute to a situation where their relationship becomes vulnerable to an extramarital affair at midlife.

Another example of a codependent hitting the wall and having a midlife crisis would be the situation of Nadine and Samuel. Nadine has a high-powered personality that is dominant and strong, but is also full of anxiety and worry. As a result, she is irritable and restless due to anxiety which comes off in a very dominant way. Nadine exudes a need to be right, to control and to overprotect. Samuel is more laid-back and tends to endure those tendencies and not share his own thoughts and then, in the process, naturally becomes more and more codependent. Samuel hit the wall and started to get involved in a variety of extracurricular activities outside of work and the home. He made the mistake that many codependents make which is to build up resentment for feeling like he wasn't doing anything wrong and his spouse was doing everything wrong. He started to compensate in a very passive-aggressive way by doing his own thing. Samuel became involved in a softball league that had regular weekend tournaments as well as a winter hockey league that practiced two nights a week and had weekend tournaments all winter long. Samuels' overcompensation due to his resentments made him unavailable for some of his children's activities. Samuel's "midlife crisis" wasn't an affair, it was unavailability. The midlife crisis for the codependent eventually hitting the wall stems from not addressing one's feelings early in life and in the marriage and allowing resentment to build up.

The Codependent Creates Boundaries & Changes the Rules

The third and final example of what may eventually occur as a result of the impact of narcissism and codependency is actually the least common; sometimes the codependent creates boundaries and changes the rules. The codependent may develop boundaries and the narcissist/controller type may change. Consider the story of Samantha and Edward. Edward grew up in an alcoholic home with a mean, drunk father. Edward made a pact with himself that he would never drink and he never did. His personality style, however, was one that was very rough emotionally. He was intimidating to his wife and their four children, he was hard on his wife and ruled the home with an iron fist. Having been controlled as a young man, Edward was going to make sure that no one controlled him as an adult. As a child, he was bullied and as an adult he became the bully. His wife Samantha grew up the oldest daughter in the home where the mother had an untreated eating disorder and lots of anxiety. Samantha's own issues with body image and eating disorders made her vulnerable to feelings of low self-esteem, perfectionism and, ultimately, codependency. Edward's harsh and shaming personality further reinforced Samantha's negative view of herself and this pattern continued for years. This was not the end of Edward and Samantha's story.

The story for this couple started to be rewritten as a friend of Samantha's one day gently confronted her on her concern with how she viewed Edward treating her. Initially Samantha minimized and defended Edward. Samantha's friend was amazing. She didn't force the issue, she set the table. She just listened to Samantha's defense and let it go for that day. Samantha did start to think about her friend's points though. One day, over six months later, Samantha went back to her friend and acknowledged that she felt overwhelmed and confused as what to do next. Samantha's friend again listened, she didn't rush to fix, manage, or problem solve, she just listened. She then asked Samantha something that hardly anybody had ever asked her: "How do you feel when Edward treats you that way?" Samantha paused and said, "I don't know...I guess overwhelmed and confused as I said earlier." Her friend replied..."Ok." " I'm so sorry for the pain you feel." "I'm here for you as a friend but, I think it would be amazing and helpful for you if you talked to a therapist who is trained to help you with something like this." Samantha said, "I'm not okay with that idea." Again, Samantha's friend just listened and said that she understood Samantha's feelings. These honest conversations however were the start of a new chapter for Samantha.

Samantha started with reading some self-help books on eating disorders and then on marriage. She started to just take in what the books were suggesting. A few months into her reading she went to her friend and said that she was more open to the idea of getting help. Her friend had done her homework. She had a few names of therapists that she had heard good things about and offered those to Samantha. Samantha did follow up on those names and eventually chose one. All this time, Samantha had kept things to herself and never discussed any of it with Edward.

After several months of therapy, Samantha started to assert herself in the marriage. She didn't try to win or be right, but rather just to let Edward know how she felt in real time. Edward's patterns didn't change at first, but he was befuddled by these "changes." As the codependent starts to find their voice, the controller/narcissistic type like Edward tends to get more agitated and more controlling to start. However, depending on the couple and the severity of the narcissistic traits of the Edwards of the world, sometimes there is a shift. Sometimes the codependent starts to gain traction and more confidence. Their confidence leads to more honesty and a sense that there is no turning back. The pattern of feeling shamed, controlled, and anxious became unacceptable as Samantha found her voice. As Samantha became more able to express herself, Edward began to feel worried, scared and out of control. Finally, Samantha said to Edward: " If we don't get help together, I think we should separate."

I will leave this story for now and eventually share later in the book some of the antidotes. Nonetheless...what this story is suggesting is, albeit much more the exception than the rule ... once in a while the codependent creates boundaries and changes the rules!

Chapter 6

ANTIDOTES

One way that the couple can improve their own relationship and create a better future for their children is to develop antidotes early in their relationship. As the name implies, antidotes help to inoculate the relationship from the potential challenges presented by both narcissistic and codependent traits. It should be noted that the development of antidotes is an intentional process that takes time and will not happen overnight. As mentioned earlier, the development of codependent and narcissistic traits often times happen early in the couple's individual stories, many times predating the couple's relationship. As such, the capacity to adjust and potentially change these long-held characteristics requires commitment to a process of healing and growth, a process that will take true effort and may well continue throughout the rest of their lives.

Antidotes for the Codependent

1. Be Truthful

Codependents tend to avoid telling the truth because they too often are defined by, or afraid of, the response of others.

In the case of Patrick and Suzanne, Suzanne's mother complained about her father and Suzanne failed to confront her mother about it despite feeling very uncomfortable, guilty about her father, etc. As a classic codependent, Suzanne then brought those same feelings into her relationship with Patrick. This is a key element in the codependent story: rather than face a confrontation with a controlling person, a codependent will default to avoidance. The key to a codependent's happiness is to be honest with both themselves and with others with whom they have relationships. The truth will either repair the relationship or will result in the end of an unhealthy relationship, either of which will contribute to a happier life.

Often the truth is seen as confrontation by the controller/narcissist and is not well received. Indeed, the fear that the controller will not receive truth well is typically the reason that the codependent avoids speaking truth. Eventually, most codependent spouses reach a point where he or she are willing to risk conflict in order to speak the truth.   When this happens, there may be conflict, but this process often creates permanent boundaries for the couple's future relationship.   In essence, the pleaser/codependent spouse has earned relational freedom by risking an uncomfortable conversation.   The codependent has often spent most of his or her life living in what I call "the house of fear"; they are immobilized by a fear of making the "wrong" decision versus the honest decision.   When the codependent speaks out in truth, they get to live more often in what I call "the house of truth"; a place where the codependent (and the controller) are able to be free to be honest with themselves and with each other.

2. Set Healthy Boundaries

Boundaries allow people to create a place to have their own feelings, to be confident and content in their own ideas. Without the boundaries, the codependent is too engaged in their partner's head, worried about what their partner thinks and feels, often over emphasizing both. I like to tell my clients that there are typically three types of boundaries that may need to be set.

Boundary #1: Honest Conversations

Honest conversations today will likely avoid harder conversations in the future. Although honesty often causes difficult conversations - maybe even conflict - today, honesty will mute harder conversations later. The honest conversation today also helps the codependent see that the issue is now on the table versus in their head. This means that as the codependent type confronts the controller in real time about something that just happened and how it made them feel; they then also get to make a request that can be anything from: 1) That action can never happen again, 2) I need to talk about the issue first or 3) Please let me know what you are feeling and let me in on that versus taking it out on me.   An honest conversation basically involves the codependent sharing with their spouse how an action made them feel and then asking them to change that action.

Honest conversations are often difficult for the codependent. Recall that codependents typically fear conflict. What often happens is that the codependent gets up the nerve to have a hard conversation. This hard conversation sometimes does not go well, perhaps it turns into a conflict situation or perhaps the codependent does not see immediate results. Often, she or he may abandon the strategy entirely because the codependent thinks that "it didn't work." What he or she often overlooks is that truthful conversation always "works", particularly when compared with avoidance. Remember that the codependent needs to pursue honesty at all costs. Honesty today prevents problems tomorrow. Most importantly then with this first boundary: Codependents are practicing inside-out behavior that sets in motion a pattern of honesty forever - there is NO turning back.

Boundary #2: Loving Detachment

More often than not, as the pleaser/codependent is setting in motion the honest conversation boundary, the controller gets more and more frustrated. Often, as the controller begins to lose control over the codependent, the controller will get more and more concerned and may begin to act out. If the environment is not safe for the codependent to move forward with this boundary ... they will need to bring in a second boundary that is called: Loving detachment...or "medium chill". In this type of boundary, the codependent asserts to self that they need emotional distance from the partner or spouse because the honest conversations continue to escalate into some type of unsafe feeling for them. By "installing" this second boundary they can live day to day with a sense of choosing to be respectful and assertive...but not emotionally close. The controller/narcissistic type may recognize this new distance and continue to be frustrated, hurt, or feel abandoned. But, the pleaser/codependent may need to assert this type of temporary boundary in order to live in a safe, day to day, environment. They don't necessarily avoid an honest conversation, but the situation may require a type of emotional separation as the couple gets help to create a safe place to have difficult discussions. In some cases, as the codependent moves into this loving detachment mode, it may cause the controller to make some changes.

Boundary #3: Separation

If the first two boundaries do not work...the codependent may need to have a physical separation from their spouse/partner. If the environment is vulnerable to abuse, this boundary is recommended. Along with this boundary, I typically recommend that the only way to re-engage together is to do so in front of a professional. In the confines of a therapy office, the couple can then be guided into some boundaries around the separation.

3. Live Inside-Out vs. Outside-in

Earlier in the chapter on codependency, I addressed the idea of living "inside-out" as opposed to "outside-in." Again, many pleaser/codependent types tend to be defined by what others think of them, in the process minimizing what they think of themselves. They can be on an endless mission of seeking validation from others. This pattern makes them vulnerable to a lack of a healthy, loving view of self and being drawn into and remaining stuck in toxic relationships. It can also lead to poor boundaries with others and make one vulnerable to emotional affairs and other poor coping mechanisms.

One common coping mechanism that a codependent deploys is the outside-in mentality; they adjust who they are based on who they are with. The outside environment determines their internal thoughts, feelings and choices. "Inside-out" is the opposite; the pleaser/codependent derives their sense of well being from their own internal feelings instead of outside influences. The beauty of instead living "inside-out" is that the codependent can start gaining awareness of their own thoughts and feelings. They can start to live from their inside out into the world with a fresh sense of freedom to be integrus and authentic. They get to be less defined by others' view of them but more defined by their own capacity to be empathetic and assertive in their actions and choices. This shift from outside-in to inside-out takes time, energy, and intentionality.

Throughout the book we have seen cases of the pleaser/codependent deferring and acquiseing mostly due to a lack of awareness of their own thoughts and feelings. Whether it was Ken, LaTasha, Samantha or others, we saw that changes and improvements can only come from within. The key to living from the inside out is to realize that the codependent's job is not to change their spouse or partner, but to change themselves!!

4. Be Accountable for Releasing Resentments

One of the most difficult struggles for codependents, especially as they near middle adulthood, is the potential truckload of resentments they are dragging around. Whether these resentments come from their upbringing, friendships, or dating/marital relationships, these weights can drag them down and make them bitter. These resentments are often built by a single event where the codependent feels that he or she has been wronged by another. The resentment then gets deposited into a figurative "bank account" which stores all of their wrongs. This is a common practice for the codependent and this pattern is one that can go on for a very long time.

The cure for this pattern is for the codependent person to be proactive in each and every situation, to know that they have a choice to assert themselves; to address the issue versus avoiding the issue. If they choose to avoid the issue, they must take responsibility for that avoidant choice versus blaming the other party for it. They may still choose to avoid conflict, but now they get to be accountable for their own actions versus blaming others for what happened. By pursuing accountability to self, they hopefully will see that they are now free to live an authentic life full of abundance to be real and to find their own voice versus the alternative!

The other proactive step for the codependent is to release resentments from the past through the power of forgiveness. Forgiveness happens over time...not overnight. Now that they are starting to see the value of setting healthy boundaries from the inside-out, hopefully they can see that they were not doing that in the past and to release past resentments slowly but surely. This action is not meant to excuse the behavior of others that have done hurtful things to them as the codependent still needs to protect themselves from those unhealthy situations. Setting boundaries is more about avoiding the bitterness that prevents oneself from living in the freedom of loving self and others in a way that is guided by honest and assertive choices versus avoidant and people pleasing tendencies. Bitterness is a weight that prevents one from living freely.

Antidotes for the Controller/Narcissistic Type

Usually I start my seminars on narcissism by saying, "If you think you're a narcissist, you're not." It is often difficult to break the chain of narcissism because a classic clinical narcissist will have a very difficult time recognizing the signs of narcissism in themselves and an even harder time hearing about the signs from another. The irony is that most people around a narcissist instantly identify his or her narcissistic tendencies, but the narcissist simply cannot see this in him or herself. Most narcissists believe that they are not narcissists. Therefore, the first step in breaking the chain of narcissism is to do what we read in recovery books: the narcissist has to believe that they have a problem. The narcissist must first acknowledge that they have an illness and that they are powerless over the problem that they have. The greatest challenge that I have confronted in my practice is that narcissists do not believe that they have a problem. The first step toward healing is for the narcissist to begin to free him or herself from narcissism; he or she needs to acknowledge that we all have problems and that he or she does as well.

1. Pursuing Healthy Attachments

As I mentioned earlier, my experience with controlling/ narcissistic types is that the roots typically go back to either a very entitled upbringing or upbringing full of shame and abandonment. It is usually one extreme or the other. Let's talk about each.

In order for a controlling/narcissistic type to be released from the feelings of shame and abandonment, he or she must understand what a healthy attachment looks like. Healthy attachment to another human being allows people to feel safe, to have conversations and to "play" in the world independently. The most secure base of attachment means just that, that the person feels safe to discuss delicate things, to enjoy other people's company and to thrive in one's own company.

The controller does not provide that for other people and is not able to provide it for themselves either. The controller must first learn to provide a secure base of attachment within themselves before they can become a base for other people. This requires the narcissist/controller to become gentle, kind to themselves and love oneself. This latter characteristic may seem contradictory as many believe that narcissists love themselves above all. This, however, is often not true. It is true that the controller is self-absorbed and controlling, but he or she often also struggles secretly with a low self esteem. One who truly loves him or herself does not usually treat other people the way that a controller/narcissist type treats people.

Instead I have found that narcissistic personalities are often born out of unfortunate and traumatic personal experience. Often narcissism is created by a background of bullying and various types of abuse. The result is that narcissists often respond to this type of upbringing by becoming bullying, dominating and abusing people themselves. To overcome this lifetime of learning, narcissists need to begin by learning how to love themselves and to develop healthy attachment with others, particularly when the narcissism arises from an upbringing of abandonment and shame. Because of the nature of the struggle, narcissists must start with small sound bites of healthy conversations both inside and outside themselves. This begins with developing healthy attachments with people who can help them to be accountable to their path towards healing.

One strategy I use as part of helping narcissists to develop healthy attachments is called "reparenting". This is a process whereby the narcissist is taught to parent themselves in a way that is healthy because they often were not parented well themselves. I work with the controller to take small steps along a path of recovery such as ending each day with words of affirmation - "this was a good day" and "here are the good choices I made today" and "here are the good choices I'm going to make tomorrow." In order for this process to work, the controller must have a therapist or other accountability partner who can help the narcissist stay on track. The key is to develop integrous relationships that are confident and content versus relationships where they are bullying or are being bullied. This process of breaking the chain of narcissism is a very slow process, but also very freeing. The controlling/narcissistic type can gradually and incrementally retake control of their own life, assessing the relationships that they have at home, at work, with friends, etc. As they begin to become more in touch with their own relationships, the narcissist must ask themselves whether those relationships are safe for the narcissist and others. In the process, the narcissist gains an appreciation for the battle. As the narcissist takes control of his or her own life, he or she is then able to start asking whether the relationships in his or her life are bringing life to both the narcissist and the other person. This process can begin an evolution that ends with more healthy attachments, more accountability and more progress toward healing.

Developing a healthy attachment for the narcissist that grew up with entitlement is even more difficult to achieve. In this situation, the narcissist is used to being coddled and entitled, leading to a lack of self-awareness of his or her dependence upon others. They grew up getting their own way and having things handed to them, but because of their personality types, they did not realize that others were doing things for them. Often, the self-entitled controller is not even open to the possibility of change. The typical entitled narcissist has a lifetime of experience where people around him or her to acquiesce to him or her. Eventually, the narcissist's friends and family will stop acquiescing to him or her. When this happens, the narcissist typically gets rid of the non-compliant friend or family member, continuing a cycle of replacing healthy attachments with compliant/codependent ones. The first antidote, then, is to create healthy attachments with others. They would need to recognize that they are not always right and that they need to increase empathy.

2. Increase Empathy ... Being FOR Others

I remember talking with somebody who was fixing my garage door. He began to talk about his personal life and it came out that he had not had interaction with his children for a long period of time. He ended up telling me that he was sad that his children had not responded to him for many years. I asked why he thought that they had not responded. He told me that he did not know, but that they had his number and never called. He knew what I did for a living and asked me what I thought. I said before you get home tonight, call each of your children and talk to them.

The narcissist thinks that it is always about other people and what they need to give to the narcissist. This type of person needs to develop small examples of empathy and understanding. This will be very hard for someone like this to achieve. This particular person perhaps had a greater need to be loved and pursued by his children than was his capacity to love and pursue his children; classic narcissistic tendencies.

Narcissists need to be willing to develop empathy. Often this is a very long process of changing from an unavailable, self-absorbed person to a more empathetic person. Based on the severity of the trauma or entitlement from their upbringing, this antidote may not be feasible for this type of individual. The process of increasing empathy starts with a slow, day to day focus of being for others. What does this look like for the narcissistic type? I have found that the best way for this to have a chance is for the controller to make a commitment to long-term therapy so that they have a place to review their actions, thoughts and feelings from week to week. They have a chance to unwind the patterns from the past and to start slowly to pursue healthy choices in the present.

41

I believe that the idea of being for others starts to help the controlling type free themselves from their sense of entitlement to be right; from their fears that lead to control and from their deep feelings of inadequacy that show up in arrogance and seeking power. This idea of being for others starts with the narcissists' spouse/partner and family. Whether it was Josie, Ali, Terrance, or others from the earlier chapters they all would need to take one day at a time. They need to start slowing the game down and in every interaction with their spouse or children, they need to finish their thoughts by asking themselves, "how does this interaction affect them?" Instead of focusing on being right, they would focus on listening only. Instead of viewing a disagreement as an attack, they would understand that the other person may see the issue differently. This is an incremental process of one conversation at a time, one day at a time and sometimes one step forward, one step back.

One of the hardest pieces for this type of person in their recovery and pursuit of being for others more is that their close family and friends may themselves be on a journey of healing; dealing with their own hurt and seeking space from the controlling person. Remember from earlier this chapter that the antidotes for codependents involve setting strong boundaries and starting to assert self more. Often, there is a strong "time zone" difference here. As part of the controller's healing path, he or she may be trying to increase empathy slowly, but this may be met with the codependent's own healing path which may feel to the controller like fierce and righteous resistance. The controller needs to be aware of this risk going into those situations and to start by understanding that the healing process will take time and consistent effort. The controller's healing path is the same whether the marriage stays together or not and whether the child forgives today, tomorrow, or not for a very long time.

The essential truth for the narcissist/controller type is that he or she gets to start to make amends for a lifetime of hurt. He or she gets to be for others versus against others and he gets to gain the need to understand others rather than the need to always be right. The tradeoff is a freedom that comes with overcoming a controlling life. By being "for" people instead of for himself or herself, the narcissist also gets to develop more supporting and truthful relationships with others. The narcissist also gets to be this way for the rest of his or her life. I believe though that for this antidote to develop and gain any traction, in addition to the commitment of long-term therapy, the controller/narcissist needs a friend or two that will hold them accountable for their actions and to stay with them through the long journey of recovery. As I mentioned earlier, way too often the controller has "yes" people around them versus people who care about them enough to challenge them when they need it!

3. Valuing & Pursuing Humility

In the spirit of one conversation at a time and one day at a time, the controller will need to gain insight into how a spirit of arrogance and a sense of coming off like a know it all is damaging to others and self. They will need to pursue the value of seeking humility and gentleness one conversation at a time and one day at a time. One of the struggles I have found with working with controlling/narcissistic types of folks is that when the mask of power and a need to be right is taken off we often find hiding beneath a scared child who needs to be validated as well. This raises the question, "What is the root truth for them?" If the controller has to receive affirmation and approval through always being told that they are right, no change has occurred. If they start to see the value of acknowledging others' feelings and listening first through a sense of humility versus a need to be recognized, then slow change may be evolving.

One of the phrases I tell the couples I see is that they get to let each other in versus take things out on each other. When couples can slowly do this from a place of mutual vulnerability versus a need to be right or liked, both people will feel safe and will enjoy more healthy attachment. So, one of the ways that this type of person can start to value and pursue humility is to let their spouse, partner, child in to what they are experiencing versus taking things out on them. As mentioned above, in addition to letting the other in, they may need to draw the other person out by asking them how they feel or how they see something. This requires intentional effort, one conversation at a time, one day at a time.

4. It's a Marathon not a Sprint!

One of the main reasons change doesn't last or occur for the controller is that they sometimes promise radical "change" out of panic borne out of the fear of losing their spouse versus changing themselves for the rest of their lives. Often we see that the codependent takes many, many years to assert himself or herself to the narcissist. By the time that he or she gets up the nerve to confront the controller, the codependent is often so frustrated that he or she feels "done" with the person, marriage or relationship. Commonly, when he or she finally hears the codependent's story, the narcissist reacts by trying to "fix" the problem by promising instant change. This promise, however, is borne out of fear, not an authentic desire to change. While the feeling of fear is normal, the type of slow change of increasing empathy and pursuing humility and being for others doesn't happen overnight. The narcissist needs to begin a long-distance run from the "house of truth" not the "house of fear." This long distance run may be full of potholes, tree branches and uneven streets but it is a run that includes changing what often is a generational pattern of dominance, being right, and seeing a home with a last word Larry or Lorraine in it. The gift that the narcissistic type gets to give to self and others is the gift of healthy remorse for their side of the street, for their stuff and to show on a daily basis a strong sense of empathy, humility and being for others.

In chapter 4 I discussed the impact of the "dance" on the children. Now I would like to focus on some antidotes that the children can implement in their lives as they grow into adulthood to help ensure that they don't repeat the dance in their story.

1. Understand Their Own Tendencies

Children that are exposed to one parent being more controlling and one parent being more people pleasing commonly choose one or the other type of tendencies to implement in their own life. After all, in general, children may not listen to their parents but they will eventually imitate them. How does a child, as they evolve into adolescence and eventually adulthood, start to realize and make adjustments for these tendencies? In my experience, the earlier they build awareness into these tendencies, the earlier they can make the necessary adjustments. The most common way they may start to gain understanding is through bumping into chronic familial conflicts. Another typical way is when they go through a relationship break-up and have some post-mortem reflections. Ideally, these reflections can come through the process of counseling. Sometimes discussing with a trusted friend or loved one who is wise about such matters can help as well.

Let's look at the case of Timon and his story. Timon grew up as the oldest male in the home. He had one older sister as well as a younger brother. Timon started to see a pattern in his parent's marriage of his mother talking over his father. His father would tend to agree with his spouse at all times. Into his late adolescent years Timon started to see that he would avoid asking a girl/young lady out because he didn't know what to say. He began to see how inadequate he felt. He noticed that he was much more concerned about whether the person appeared to like him versus whether he was drawn to that person. Timon also noticed that several of his friends didn't appear to have the same issue in pursuing dating relationships. Timon's feelings of inadequacy started to discourage him greatly. He also developed some significant depressive symptoms, so his mother got him in to see a therapist after his first year of college.

In the therapeutic process, Timon started to see how he had picked up on his father's avoidant tendencies and was living that out. He also noticed that his fear of addressing a conflict with his mother was leading to him spending way too much time in the other lady's head perseverating about what she may or may not be thinking about him and reacting much more to his interpretation of her cues versus his own thoughts and feelings. Timon became aware of the importance of knowing his own feelings and the importance of looking at his goals and values in life rather than focusing on his fears.

Timon decided to implement some of these changes as he went back to college. Initially he struggled with some of the same fears and feelings. But over time, he started to gain insight into how much fear he had and how much power he was giving to it. Thankfully, Timon developed tools that continued in counseling for several years that made him develop a much more assertive, self-confident view of self and that was key in his exploration of pursuing a dating relationship.

The story of Timon is one that exemplifies how the life of a pleaser type of personality can make adjustments in their story due to increased awareness of their tendencies. How about an individual young adult who may be vulnerable to the tendencies of a controller type? Let's look at the story of Megan. Megan sought out therapy in her mid 20's after going through a tough break up with her fiance'. Megan's parents had the same dance as Timon's. A controlling mom and a passive father. Unlike Timon, Megan was the first born. From the start in Megan's life she pursued life with gusto and a direct posture. She tended to get what she wanted because she made things happen. Sounds good so far ... the potential trouble for the Megan's of the world occur when they bring this personality, unfiltered, into a romantic relationship. Megan met her fiance' Keith after college at work. Both worked on similar projects in a company so they were running into each other a lot. Megan noticed Keith and pursued him actively. Keith was flattered by the pursuit and responded well to it and their dating relationship developed. For two plus years they grew in their relationship and eventually fell in love with each other. Megan, after these two plus years, became impatient with Keith's tendencies to avoid. To Megan's credit, she pointed this out to Keith and he would acknowledge his struggle to bring things up that he thought Megan would disagree with. What Keith wasn't saying was that Megan's need to be right; her capacity to interrupt him, speak for him, and direct him was wearing on him. Keith began to build a resentment bank account and began making regular deposits. Like many controllers, Megan did not see the building conflict.

Megan and Keith's story continues with their engagement. Keith broke off their engagement soon after the date for their wedding was set. Naturally, Megan was crushed. Keith felt bad for hurting Megan, but he did not re-enter the relationship. He was done. Megan sought out therapy due to residual grief, deep hurt and feelings of rejection. Initially, Megan was just blaming Keith for his choice to run away and not deal with the issues; a common way for a controller to cope with relational pain. After a while in therapy, however, Megan began to do her own work and consider her own part of the story. She started to see that she had a capacity to steamroll people and that this was especially true in her romantic relationships. She also learned how these tendencies started and how some of her amazing strengths to get after life and make things happen have served her well. She also learned the art of being more mindful; of slowing down emotionally to create safe spaces with her best friends and future dating partner(s) to have dialogue. To give and take. To listen to understand. As Megan grew in this awareness, she also learned to see the similarities she had with her mother. All of the strengths but the blindspots as well.

2. Be Careful not to Overcompensate for their Past

The stories of Megan and Timon show how when two young adults look at their tendencies and make adjustments there can be a full life to be lived. Unfortunately, children with a narcissistic and codependent parent will often overcompensate for their upbringing, especially as they are growing into their romantic relationships. These children may clearly see the faults of the codependent parent, for example, and decide that they do not want to be like the codependent parent. The challenge is that, in the process of avoiding the codependent traits, they become vulnerable to adopting the personality traits of the more controlling parent, and vice versa. Here are a couple of examples to consider: First let's look at the story of Maggie.

Maggie grew up in a home with an alcoholic father who also cheated on her mother. Maggie witnessed her father be emotionally abusive to her mother and eventually left her and the family for another woman. Maggie watched her mother endure the abuse and the betrayal and was devastated by it. Maggie was the oldest in her family of five with two younger brothers. Maggie had some of her mother's pleasing tendencies and often looked for her father's approval throughout her upbringing. Maggie also provided support for her mother through the betrayal process. Maggie's pleasing tendencies also showed up in her friendships as she would help her friends as they were going through hard times and generally was the giver in these relationships.

Predictably Maggie endured some unhealthy relationships with other boys in high school and young men in her college and early work years. She wasn't necessarily drawn to the types of males that reminded her of her father, but she endured these types. Eventually she eventually met Anthony at work. Anthony was kind, empathetic and had a fair amount of pleasing tendencies. They got married. Early in their marriage, even though they would have some drinks as a couple when they dated, Maggie started to get very agitated whenever Anthony would have some wine with dinner at home. Although neither had a pattern of overuse, during their fifth year of marriage, Anthony had too much to drink while they were out with friends. This really impacted Maggie and she began to notice whenever they would have anything to drink as a couple. Maggie also began to notice if Anthony had any interaction with one of her friends or with a female at work. Even though Anthony's boundaries with women were good, Maggie started to accuse him of cheating on her and of being an alcoholic. Neither of her accusations were true, but the trauma she had vicariously experienced through her mother and father trumped the truth. Maggie became vulnerable, as many do who grow up with this type of trauma, to overcompensating for her past. Her people pleasing tendencies were now starting to be replaced with a few narcissistic tendencies. The need to be right. The need to expect automatic compliance to her wishes. A lack of empathy and making demands versus requests. This overcompensating felt right to Maggie and gave her a way of coping with the past so the little girl, young lady that was exposed to the horrific things her father did to her mother could now make sure that that never happened to her. Her self-protection was actually an overcorrection that was due to her past, not to who Anthony was.

Let's look at another story. The story of Clayton and his upbringing is similar to Timon's. Clayton noticed that his mother would always be correcting and parenting his father. His father would endure this type of treatment and would go out of his way to try and keep his mother happy just to avoid the drama. Like Maggie, Clayton had significant tendencies to please. He, like Timon, avoided a lot of dating situations due to his inability to feel confident in himself. He was the best friend of several girls in high school and women at work in his adult life. He was set up on a blind date by a friend (yes sometimes they can work out) with a wonderful young woman named Bernice. Bernice was assertive, smart, and had a healthy level of confidence and self-efficacy. After struggling with a year and a half of not being sure about a commitment, he did propose to Bernice and she accepted.

In their first year of marriage Clayton's overcompensation began. Whenever Bernice would express her feelings about an issue, and especially when she would share some disappointment she had with Clayton about something that happened; Clayton would get irritated. He couldn't believe that she would bring up her concerns. He interpreted her sharing her hurt feelings as an attack on his character. He knew how his father endured being treated by his mother and he was going to be darn sure no spouse treated him that way! Like Maggie, Clayton saw his life experience through the lens of trauma. Although his anger and hurt were real feelings, the connection between his feelings and Bernice's actions was not accurate. Clayton's personal trauma trumped what was true.

Clayton's need to avoid confrontation created a space for Bernice that wasn't emotionally safe. Instead of learning from his past and trying to see the value of healthy asserting of feelings in good times AND in conflicts and disagreements; he was overcompensating for his past and clearly was in need for some adjustment in his thinking and eventually in his feelings and choices.

One key takeaway here is that it is crucial to know one's tendencies, but also to be very careful not to overcompensate for issues from the past. Often times when one does overcompensate, they turn into the parent they didn't want to become! The other key takeaway is that when one is overcompensating for their past it often takes a long time for it to be noticed! Remember that, in general, when one is overcompensating for trauma, one will have a tendency to be easily enraged, have significant times of shutting down and have a strong negative bias in their thinking about their partner/spouse. So, while this overcompensating is happening, it is usually putting the spouse/partner on their heels and will potentially make them vulnerable to being codependent, even a spouse who is himself or herself narcissistic. It is a sad reality that overcompensation can shift family roles and can even turn a codependent spouse into a severely narcissistic personality type.

3. Look for what they are For in the Development of their Identity

Most people who grow up in the dynamic of narcissism and codependency end up defining themselves by what they are against rather than what they are for. Most such people live in avoidance, the fear of not wanting to repeat the past they saw, instead of and active and intentional pursuit of a healthy and abundant life. So far we have learned that the antidotes for the children that grow up experiencing the "dance" include being aware of their own tendencies and being careful not to overcompensate for their past. Now they get to lean into what they are for, not what they are against.

Consider the story of Zach. Zach pursued counseling in his 30's after a very difficult break up. Zach unpacked his story of growing up with a demanding father who needed to be right along with a passive "go along to get along" mother. Zach, generally wired like his mother, would agree with dad whatever the cost. Zach would come home from school and when his father would get home from work, Zach would take his father's emotional temperature, which would determine Zach's approach to the evening. That would help Zach decide if he could ask to use the car; whether he could stay out just a little bit later than normal and more importantly, whether Zach or his mother or sister would be yelled at that night. Like a true budding codependent, Zach knew others, but didn't know self.

Zach's long term love interest, Gabriella, grew up with a strong sense of entitlement and generally got what she wanted. This worked well for Zach as he deferred to "Gabby" regularly in their day to day interactions and decisions. Over the years however, Gabby grew weary of Zach's indecisiveness and how controlled he was by his father. Gabby lost respect for Zach and regularly broke up with him. These break-ups were horrific to Zach. The pleaser in him was crushed and defined by her moods and choices. After their potential "last" break-up, Zach finally reached out to get some help. He got his counselor's name from a work friend who had had a good experience with this particular counselor.

In Zach's counseling he started to learn of his family's dynamics as well as his own "dance" with Gabby. Zach was ruminating on how awful his father was and how that was the demise of him and Gabby. Zach was losing energy slowly each day because his identity was being shaped by what his father had done to his mother and that Gabby didn't approve of him either. Naturally those chronic difficult experiences of his upbringing and the back and forth with Gabby were feeling overwhelming to Zach. Through the counseling process, however, the shift moved from what had happened to him to what he now gets to do for himself. Sure, good learning can come from ensuring that he doesn't repeat the dance of mom and dad and that he doesn't get into another Gabby hurricane. But, also what worked for Zach was for him to start to evaluate his own values. He needed to understand what HE valued, what he found HE found lovely, beautiful, life-giving, abundant, and pure. Drawing from the inside-out work discussed earlier in the book, Zach slowly gained momentum in looking at his friendships, his boundaries with his family, pursuing what he valued most which was a sense of adventure, wonder, and being for giving to others. The giving to others shifted from not a need to please others but rather to give from a place of confidence and strength to those in need. For Zach, that came through his avocational life. His vocational life brought him financial security, but it didn't bring him deep fulfillment. Zach didn't have to change his personality and become a bully to others because he was bullied by his father and to some extent his dance with Gabby. Instead, he found that he could feed the beautiful parts of being FOR himself and others by volunteering with two different organizations that brought hope to people with no hope.

This early life adjustment for Zach involved him being committed to the counseling process and redirecting his pleasing tendencies into not seeking validation from others but instead being altruistic toward others and much more gentle toward self. This also helped him meet a handful of people who became good friends in his story as his best friends became people who, like Zach, have the capacity to give love and receive it as well.

Another example comes from Carlita's story. She experienced a lot of abandonment as a young woman, mostly by her mother. Her mother left her, her father and five siblings when she was an early teen. This abandonment and her father's resulting absence due to working three jobs, left her fending for things on her own a lot. Thankfully she experienced success at school. She was tremendously gifted in theatre and athletics. She received accolades for her hard work and consistent performances. Even though these were helpful in her early story, the cloud of abandonment was heavy. She tended to endure difficult relationships with boys and eventually married in her early 20's. She, like her father, worked very hard. She became pregnant within two years of her marriage to Ricardo and had three children in five years. Ricardo, like her father, was an absent father. Ricardo's absence was due to liquor and womanizing, not work.

Carlita endured this dance of plowing through her days of work, getting her kids ready for school, picking them up after school, feeding them, getting them to bed. By her mid 30's, Carlita was growing weary of the same routine, day after day. She found Ricardo in the arms of another woman one night at home when she and the kids came home unexpectedly early from a summer trip. That was the final straw for Carlita. She certainly wasn't going to abandon her family as her mother did, although she thought about it once or twice during her worst days. Through some good advice from a wise friend, she protected herself from Ricardo's on-going dysfunction and pursued a divorce. The divorce was hard on her and everyone involved. It certainly wasn't her first choice being a person of strong faith. But she knew that she did not want a part of Ricardo's dysfunctional patterns.

It was through the divorce process that Carlita was able to consider, for the first time, what she valued in her life. She had basically been in survival mode for all of thirty some years. Now it was her turn to pursue life instead of merely surviving. For her, it started for her by being the best parent she could be to her kids and that included her working hard; loving them well and being present for them. She realized that she could develop a new identity and that through her new identity she could pursue what she was for, instead of running from what she was against. She realized that she was for laughter, developing good friends, and getting back to some of what brought her joy earlier in her story which included theatre. She joined the community theatre and surrounded herself with good people from her faith community and she started to thrive in life. She started to experience what she was for in life versus what she had to do to survive. Slowly, but surely, through friends, faith, family, and acting....her life became rich. By pursuing what she was for, it also helped her have strong boundaries with her former partner Ricardo. Instead of perseverating about his destructive choices, she started to dwell on the individuality of each of her children and their stories and to breathe into them versus being exhausted by Ricardo's choices.

4. THE NEW DANCE

The most exciting antidote to discuss is the opportunity for children who have grown up being exposed to the dance to begin their own new dance. A dance that involves their own thoughts, feelings, and choices. An opportunity to learn from their past instead of being defined by it. Like all antidotes, this one requires intentionality and being steadfast in the journey. The areas of value and meaning that it can bring, however, have the potential to be transformational to the individual and to their loved ones.

Let's look at the key ingredients then to this new dance as these children potentially enter into a marriage of their own.

Ingredient #1 - Mutual Vulnerability

I have discussed the idea of a couple learning to "let each other in versus taking things out on each other" as a key cog in solidifying a lifelong sustainable and fulfilling relationship. When each person allows their partner to hear their own thoughts and feelings from a place of being transparent and non-blaming, it creates a safe place together. Regardless of the issue discussed; whether the couple is on the same page or not, it gives them the best opportunity to not have a need to be right or a need to be liked. Rather, it allows both to listen to understand versus listen to defend.

This process is fluid. It is on-going. There are fits and starts with it. But, if the couple is committed to it, it will change their level of intimacy and trust for each other. Many times, couples in difficult moments both can feel that they are against each other rather for each other. This is because both feel attacked instead of encouraged. Often neither spouse feels as if the other is listening to them and that their feelings are not being considered, heard or validated. Instead, being "right" is the main thing. It is often more important to get the last word in rather than working together to figure out the challenge that the couple faces.

51

Ingredient #2 - Accept each other's Differences

For most couples engaged in the dance of control and pleasing, there is an on-going process of trying to change each other. The controller is parenting the pleaser and the pleaser is wishing the controller would listen and understand. To be sure, there are unacceptables in marriages. Affairs, untreated addiction, and abuse. These areas need to be addressed when they are there. But, in relationships without these issues, there needs to be a general acceptance of different styles. One is an introvert and one is an extravert. One likes to have a plan and one likes to be in the moment. One likes to start things one likes to finish things. It goes on and on. Most couples try to change each other's styles instead of understanding that in these areas of life, people are not intentionally trying to be annoying, they are just being themselves. Healthy couples, when having these types of differences try to use the strengths of each others' styles to excel versus demanding change from each other. One of the biggest complaints I hear from couples I have worked with over the years is that they feel judged and not accepted by their spouse. The new dance involves knowing oneself well and what tendencies one has and through that sense of self-confidence, be understanding and aware of one's partners' tendencies and to be accepting of them, especially when they differ from one's own!

Ingredient #3 - Both Work on their own Side of the Street

Very quickly in marriage, individuals know what is wrong with their spouse. They develop a list, either in their head or out loud to their partner, about these areas of deficiency. The blame game starts. In my work as a Professor I teach a class on Social Psychology. In this class we discuss "self-serving bias" which we all have to some degree. It is usually very loud in marriage. The bias means that you and I tend to take credit for our successes and blame others (especially our spouse if we have a partner) for our failures. This bias invades marriages and slowly erodes love. If I'm working on my side of the street only....I've got the best chance to grow and be a healthy partner. If I'm score keeping, therapizing, parenting, and fixing my spouse....my eyes are not on the right area. There is a scripture verse that suggests that you and I should take the log out of our own eye first before judging someone else.

This is NOT to say that couples should avoid sharing their hurts and concerns. Remember that in the new dance, mutual vulnerability is key. Letting each other in versus taking things out on each other needs to be paramount. Couples that grow as individuals and as a couple, however, are committed to working on their own side of the street. Letting each other in to what they are seeing in themselves. Sharing our own fears, inadequacies, and struggles.

The best way to be able to work on our own side of the street is too slow down enough each day and to be mindful and present with our thoughts, feelings, and choices. Just like a golfer only gets better by going to the driving range a few times a week and hitting a few buckets of balls while visualizing their process; individuals need to go to their own driving range frequently to meditate, pray, and reflect on what they are feeling, what they are thinking, what are their choices, and what they are for.

In my opinion, the best part of the new dance is that the need to be right and the need to be liked are both muted. What becomes loud is two people coming toward each other with mutual vulnerability and letting each other in versus taking things out on each other!

ENJOY THE JOURNEY!!!